Addresses

Wonder Woman and all related characters, names and indicia
are trademarks of DC Comics © 1999
All rights reserved.
Wonder Woman created by William Moulton Marston.

Design by Chip Kidd and Chin-Yee Lai
Photographs by Geoff Spear
Manufactured in China

CHRONICLE BOOKS

85 Second Street, San Francisco, CA 94105
www.chroniclebooks.com

ISBN: 0-8118-2478-0

Distributed in Canada by Raincoast Books
8680 Cambie Street, Vancouver, B.C. V6P 6M9

10 9 8 7 6 5

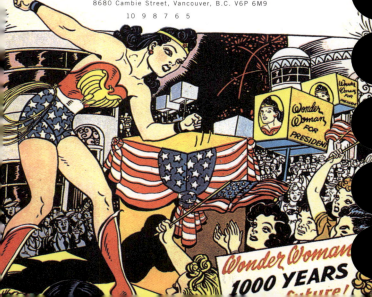

WHILE WONDER WOMAN is entirely new as a daily newspaper strip, it has long enjoyed tremendous popularity with more than 10,000,000 readers of comic books.

In a recent survey made in the city of Hudson, N.Y. among 1125 families WONDER WOMAN was first of 135 comic book characters tested with girls of from 8 to 17 years and second with adult women.

Thus, WONDER WOMAN comes to you as a new and entirely different newspaper feature, but with 10,000,000 ardent fans following her daring exploits and adventures.

FEATURES SYNDICATE

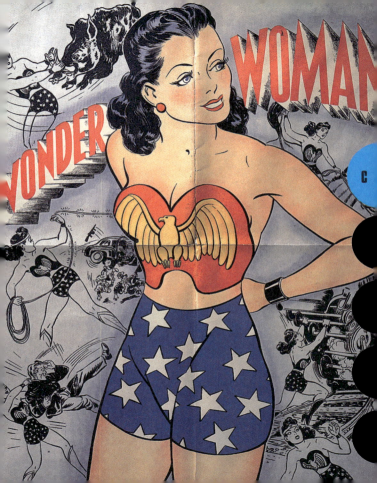

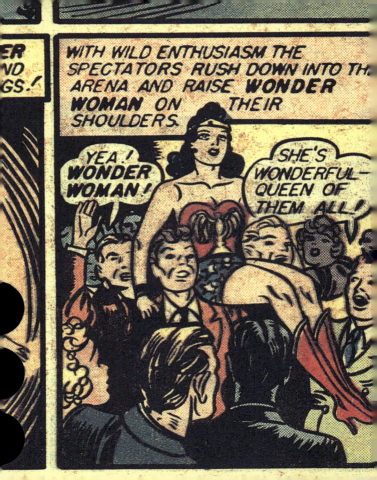

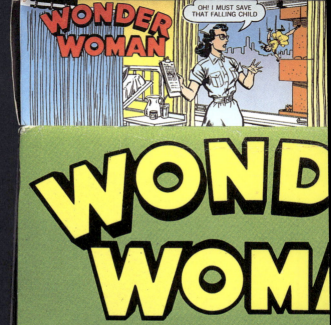

9853-3

© 1967 IDEAL TOY CORPORATION

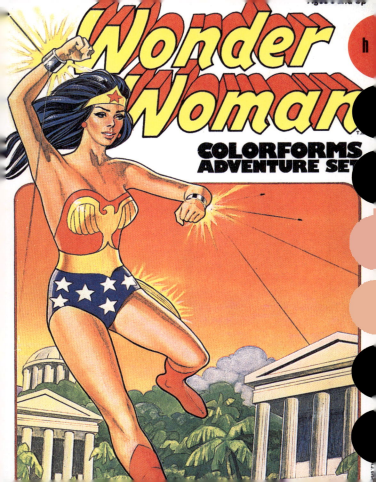

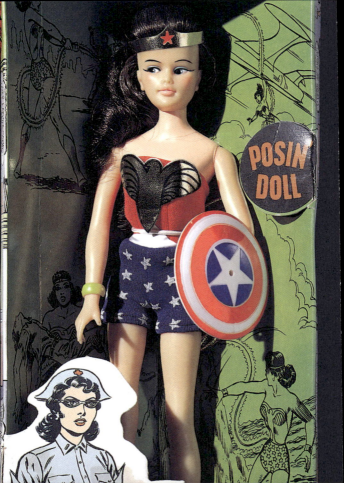

k

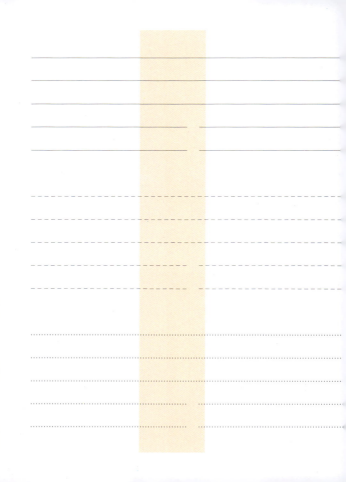

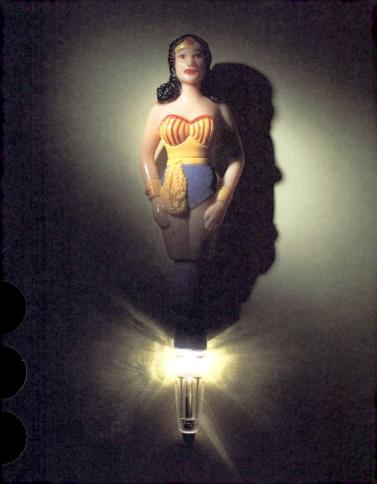

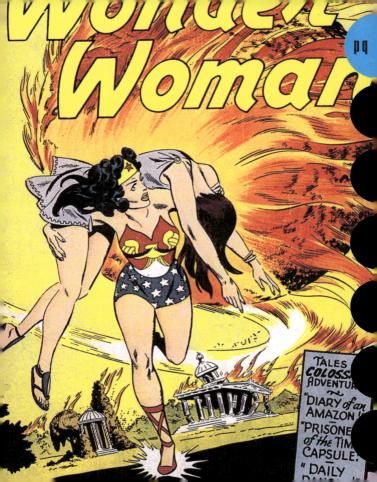

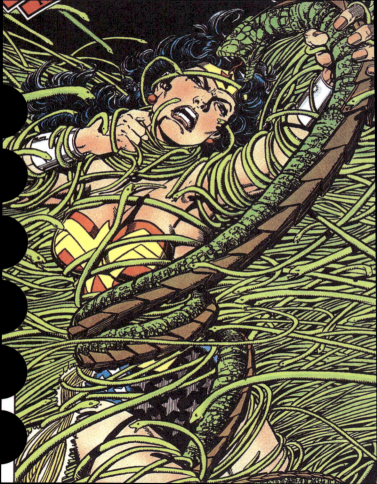

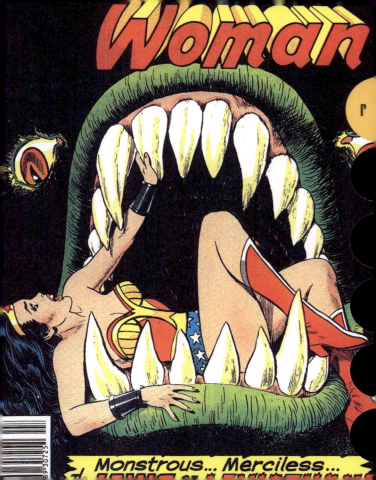

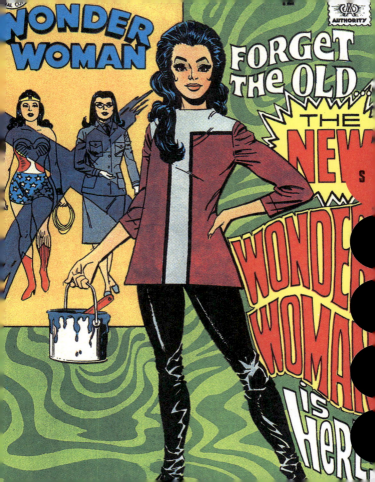

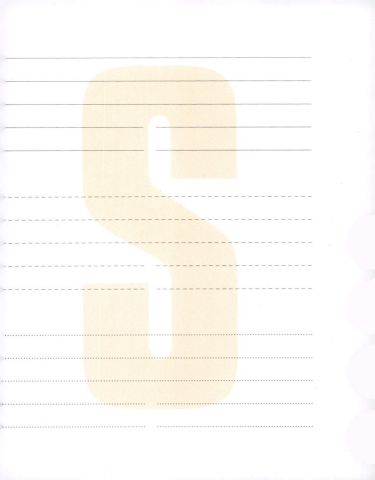